W9-ARJ-747

CANADA

the culture

Bobbie Kalman

A Bobbie Kalman Book
The Lands, Peoples, and Cultures Series

Crabtree Publishing Company

www.crabtreebooks.com

The Lands, Peoples, and Cultures Series

Created by Bobbie Kalman

For Suzanne and Caroline, who love theater, opera, and art

Written by
Bobbie Kalman

Coordinating editor
Ellen Rodger

Editor
Jane Lewis

Contributing editors
Carrie Gleason
Heather Macrae

Editors/first edition
Janine Schaub
David Schimpky
Lynda Hale

Production coordinator
Rose Gowsell

Design and production
Text Etc.

Separations and film
Quadratone Graphics Ltd.

Printer
Worzalla Publishing Company

Photographs
Charlottetown Festival/Anne of Green Gables: p. 14; Cirque du Soleil/Al Seib: p. 15 (bottom); CP Picture Archive: Kevin Frayer p. 17 (bottom), Paul Henry p. 16 (top), Tibor Kelly, p. 16 (top); Corbis/ Magmaphoto: Bettmann p. 21 (top), Mitchell Gerber p. 21 (bottom), Kelly-Mooney Photography p. 15 (top), Earl & Nazima Kowall p. 22 (left), Bob Krist p. 11, Gunter Marx p. 7 (top), Buddy Mays p. 18 (bottom), Neal Preston p. 17 (top); Reuters Newmedia Inc.: p. 17 (middle), 22 (right), Lee Snider p. 19, Paul A. Souders p. 28 (bottom); Marc Crabtree: p. 5 (top left and bottom), 13 (top), 28 (top); Betty Crowell: p. 10 (top); Ken Faris: p. 24 (right); Anne Gordon/Anne Gordon Images: p. 5 (top right), 6 (left), 7 (bottom), 8 (top), 23 (bottom); Industry, Science, and Technology Canada: p. 4 (bottom); Wolfgang Kaehler: title page, p. 6 (right), 27 (bottom), 29 (both); Terrance Klassen: p. 27 (top); Diane Payton Majumdar: p. 12 (both), 24 (left); Bob Munsch Enterprises: p. 18 (top); Phil Norton: p. 4 (top), 8 (bottom); Michael O'Connor: p. 10 (bottom); Ontario Ministry of Tourism and Recreation: p. 26; Ron Schroeder: p. 9, 20; Theatre Beyond Words: p. 13 (bottom); Weir Collection, Queenston, Ontario: *Early Canadian Settler*: p. 25 (top), *Sketch for the Jack Pine*: p. 25 (bottom); other images by Digital Stock

Every effort has been made to obtain the appropriate credit and full copyright clearance for all images in this book. Any oversights, despite Crabtree's greatest precautions, will be corrected in future editions.

Illustrations
Kristi Frost: pp. 30-31; Scott Mooney: icons; David Wysotski, Allure Illustrations: back cover

Cover: Native peoples on the west coast of Canada are known for their carved totem poles.

Title page: The streets of historic Québec City, Canada's oldest city, have a European flavor.

Icon: The maple leaf is a famous Canadian symbol that appears on the Canadian flag.

Back cover: Caribou are large deerlike animals that roam Canada's north.

Published by
Crabtree Publishing Company

PMB 16A,
350 Fifth Avenue
Suite 3308
New York
N.Y. 10118

612 Welland Avenue
St. Catharines
Ontario, Canada
L2M 5V6

73 Lime Walk
Headington
Oxford OX3 7AD
United Kingdom

Cataloging in Publication Data
Kalman, Bobbie, 1947-
    Canada. The culture / Bobbie Kalman.-- Rev. ed.
    p. cm. -- (The lands, peoples, and cultures series)
    Includes index.
    ISBN 0-7787-9360-5 (RLB) -- ISBN 0-7787-9728-7 (pbk.)
    1. Canada--Civilization--1945- .--Juvenile literature. I.
Title. II. Series.
    F1021.2 .K34 2002
    971.064--dc21

                                        2001032528
                                        LC

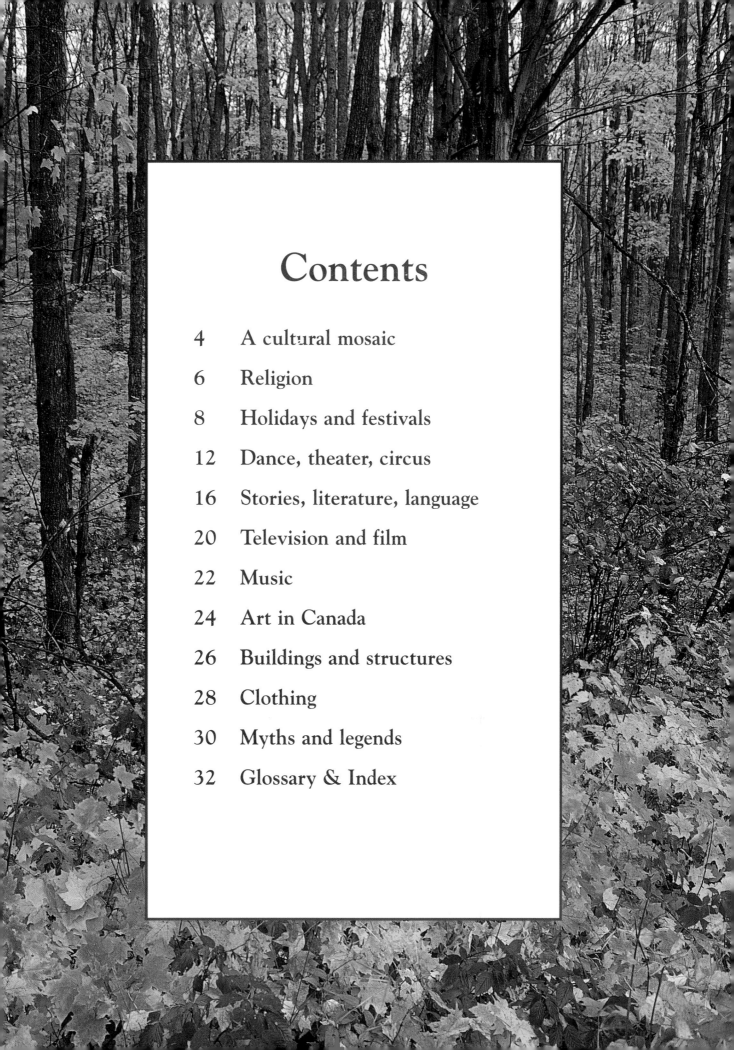

Contents

4   A cultural mosaic

6   Religion

8   Holidays and festivals

12   Dance, theater, circus

16   Stories, literature, language

20   Television and film

22   Music

24   Art in Canada

26   Buildings and structures

28   Clothing

30   Myths and legends

32   Glossary & Index

A cultural mosaic

Culture is the way people live. It is the food they eat, the clothes they wear, the stories they tell or write, the buildings they build, the dances they perform, the music they enjoy, the religious beliefs they follow, and the sports they play or watch. Culture also includes customs, **traditions**, religious celebrations, and festivals.

A mixed heritage

Thousands of years before the country of Canada existed, its land was inhabited by native peoples. The native peoples had their own languages, customs, religions, and arts. French explorers arrived in the sixteenth century and brought with them the customs and beliefs of France. The British came one hundred years after the French and had the greatest and longest-lasting influences on Canadian culture.

Global influences

Over the last few centuries, **immigrants** have come to Canada from all over the world. Newcomers from places such as China, India, Africa, Eastern Europe, and South America have brought new customs and traditions to add to Canada's **cultural mosaic**. Their contributions have influenced Canadian theater, music, literature, art, **architecture**, food, and dress.

*(above) Canadians are proud of their heritage. This picture shows both the Canadian flag, with a red maple leaf, and the Quebec flag, with the **fleur-de-lis**.*

(left) Many of Canada's native groups use masks in their traditional ceremonies. These masks represent supernatural beings.

South of the border

Canada has also been influenced by its southern neighbor, the United States. Due to the free flow of information between the two countries, some aspects of American culture have been adopted by Canadians. Many popular movies, television programs, music, fashion, and trends originate south of the border.

(this page) Asian, Scottish, and Greek influences are just a few examples of Canada's global flavor.

Support for culture

In recent years, Canadians have begun to realize the importance of maintaining a distinct culture, apart from the United States. The Canadian Government **grants** money to institutions and businesses that preserve and promote Canadian culture. Government support ensures that Canadian literature, music, art, and theater will continue to thrive.

A blend of traditions

Canada's culture is a blend of traditions and customs from around the world. The Canadian government officially honors **multiculturalism**. As a result, Canadians try to respect cultural differences. These cultural differences make Canada a rich and fascinating country.

5

Religion

Almost every religion in the world is represented in Canada. Canadians with different religious backgrounds are encouraged to follow their own faiths and traditions.

The first peoples

Native Canadians have had their own traditional beliefs for thousands of years. There are 600 **bands**, or groups, of native peoples in Canada. Each band has its own unique spiritual beliefs and practices. Many Native Canadians do not think of their spirituality as a religion, but simply as a part of who they are. There are some common threads among all native spiritual traditions. Native spirituality is closely connected to nature. All creatures and all natural things, such as trees, rivers, and mountains, are thought to be alive and have spirit. Native **shamans** are able to communicate between the natural and the spiritual world. Native people believe that all living things are interconnected and see the planet as Mother Earth. The power that made all living things is called The Creator. All bands have a version of an image called the Medicine Wheel, which represents the universe and the cycle of life.

Christian groups

Roman Catholicism, a **denomination** of **Christianity**, was first practiced in Canada by French settlers. Irish Catholics settled in Canada in the nineteenth century. Early settlers from England and Scotland introduced Protestant beliefs to Canada. Protestantism is also a Christian denomination. Today, 42 percent of Canada's population follow the Catholic religion. Protestants are the second largest group. They make up about 40 percent of the population.

The Jesuits

In the seventeenth century, a group of Roman Catholic priests called Jesuits came from France to spread the Christian religion. The Jesuits wrote letters to one another, telling of native culture. These letters were compiled into books, called *Jesuit Relations*. The books tell about the way Native Canadians lived before European settlers arrived in Canada.

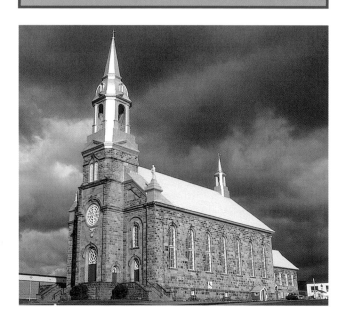

(above) Christian churches can be found in large and small communities across Canada.

(left) A Ukranian church with its distinctive domed roof.

Religious communities

Some rural areas of Canada have small communities of Amish, Mennonites, and Hutterites. These Christian groups maintain traditional religious beliefs in the midst of a modern world. These people live primarily on farms and manage without automobiles and most machinery, and dress simply in dark colors. The Amish do not even have buttons on their clothes. Mennonites are known for their beautiful bed quilts, their simple, well-made furniture, and their commitment to charity.

A variety of beliefs

Today, just over one percent of Canada's population is Jewish. The Jewish religion is over 4000 years old and based on the belief that there is only one God. The cities of Montréal and Toronto have the largest Jewish populations. More recent immigrants to Canada have brought religions such as **Hinduism**, **Islam**, **Sikhism**, and **Buddhism**.

(above) This Buddhist temple in British Columbia serves many Asian Canadians and other Buddhists.

(above) These Mennonite women are having a quilting bee, which gives them a chance to enjoy one another's company while making a quilt.

Canadians celebrate national and religious holidays, as well as numerous cultural festivals. Banks, government offices, stores, and schools are closed on national holidays. Victoria Day is a national holiday celebrated on May 24 in honor of England's Queen Victoria. Originally, this holiday was established as a way of saluting Canada's ties with the British Empire. Today, the holiday marks the beginning of summer with barbecues, fireworks, and parades. Another national holiday in Canada is Labor Day, which is held on the first Monday in September. Some widely celebrated religious holidays are Christmas, Easter, Hanukkah, Rosh Hashanah, Chinese New Year, and Holi. Canadians enjoy their holidays and celebrate with enthusiasm.

(this page) Canadian flags and symbols can be seen all over the country on Canada Day!

Canada Day

A Canadian celebration occurs across the country on July 1 each year. This national holiday marks the day in 1867 that Canada was officially declared a dominion, or self-governing nation. The holiday, originally called Dominion Day, is celebrated with barbecues, parties, and fireworks.

La Fête Nationale

La Fête Nationale is celebrated in Québec on June 24. French settlers brought the holiday to Canada in the 1600s. Originally called St. Jean Baptiste Day, it was a Christian celebration with a feast and a bonfire. It gradually lost its religious significance and became a celebration of French culture in Québec. St Jean Baptiste Day was renamed La Fête Nationale and declared the official national holiday of Québec in 1977. The holiday is now marked with family gatherings, traditional meals, bonfires, parades, and fireworks.

Thanksgiving

Canadian Thanksgiving occurs on the second Monday in October. It is believed that a combination of three historical traditions gave rise to this holiday. The first was a fall harvest celebration by European farmers. The second was Martin Frobisher, an early explorer, who gave thanks for surviving his journey to the shores of Canada. The third was the American Thanksgiving. In 1621, American pilgrims celebrated their first harvest in the New World. In 1750, this celebration was carried into Nova Scotia. These three pieces of history are the foundation of the Thanksgiving holiday celebrated in Canada today.

Holi

Holi is an East Indian festival of colors, which falls one day after the full moon in early March. It is a celebration of the changing of the seasons. People of East Indian descent in Canada celebrate Holi by saying goodbye to winter and welcoming the arrival of spring. They get together to share a meal and mark the event by hurling water mixed with brightly colored dyes at one another.

The Winnipeg Folk Festival

The Winnipeg Folk Festival lasts for three days in July. It is held at Bird's Hill Park in Winnipeg, and is the largest folk festival in the country. A folk festival was traditionally a chance for people to show their talents in the community. Today, folk festivals attract people from around the country and feature music, crafts, and food.

Montréal

Montréal hosts the Just For Laughs comedy festival each year in July. This bilingual festival features over 200 performers and draws about half a million people every year. The Montréal International Jazz Festival also takes place every summer. It features 2000 jazz musicians, and lasts for fourteen days.

(below) Québec City's Winter Carnival, or Carnaval de Québec, is a popular event that sees almost one million visitors every February. Warmly dressed participants can view ice sculptures, parades, food, and music. They can also take part in sports such as skating, skiing, hockey, and even dogsled racing! The Carnival also has a mascot—a large snowman called Bonhomme.

Canadian Dragon Boat Festival

Dragon boat racing began in the Hunan province of China about 2500 years ago. In recent years, racing the colorful boats has become popular in Canada. Now there are annual competitions in many major Canadian cities. Schools, companies, and organizations form teams and race against one another for fun, competition, and charity.

Caribana

Caribana is one of the largest cultural festivals in Canada. This celebration was started in 1967, the 100th anniversary of Canada to acknowledge the role that Caribbean culture has played in making Canada a multicultural country. The event lasts for eighteen days every summer in Toronto. During the annual Caribana grand parade, the city is filled with hundreds of thousands of people celebrating Caribbean culture. Music, bands, food, and competitions delight the festival's visitors. One of the many interesting parts of the festival is the music. The sounds of steelpan bands mix with oldstyle calypso, lively soca, and reggae – all forms of music that originated in the Caribbean.

(above) Asian cultures are represented in this Calgary parade.

(opposite page) Elaborate costumes can be seen at Toronto's Caribana festival. Prizes are awarded every year for the best costumes.

(above) This Canadian dragon boat team is made up of people who are raising money for cancer research.

🍁 Dance, theater, circus 🍁

The performing arts are an important part of Canada's culture. Dance, theater, and the circus are ways that Canadians can express their culture artistically. The Canadian tradition of performing arts began thousands of years ago with native celebrations. It continues to grow and change as new immigrant groups add their own styles of performing every year.

Cultural dancing

The native peoples of Canada use dance as a part of religious ceremonies. The dances have many purposes, such as healing the sick, celebrating a successful hunt, or praying to the spirits. Dance is also used to express identity and **heritage**. Africans and East Indians have introduced their ancestral forms of dance and lively music to Canada. Ancient Asian dances, Irish dances, and energetic European polkas are all part of Canadian dance.

(top) This energetic African-Canadian performance was part of a multicultural festival.

(right) This type of Indian dancing is called Bharata Natyam. The movements represent different human emotions.

Performing arts

Dance performances can be seen throughout Canada. Ballet, tap, jazz, and modern dance are all popular. Musical plays also allow dancers to show off their talents. Audiences have been thrilled by the performances of Canadian ballet legends, such as Karen Kain. One of the more famous troupes is the National Ballet of Canada. Founded in 1951, the National Ballet has earned international praise for its performances.

Canadian theater

Big cities such as Toronto, Ottawa, Montréal, Winnipeg, and Vancouver have many theaters that showcase the talents of Canadian actors, dancers, and musicians. Many smaller cities have community theater groups where members can showcase their talents performing well-known plays and musicals.

(above) Many Canadian children enjoy taking lessons in tap, jazz, and ballet. The National Ballet School of Canada, located in Toronto, provides ballet training for many future dancers.

(left) Theatre Beyond Words is a creative theater group that combines the art of mime with colorful costumes and exciting music.

13

Charlottetown Festival

In the summer of 1965, the first production of the musical *Anne of Green Gables* was performed in Charlottetown, Prince Edward Island. This musical play is based on a popular novel by Lucy Maud Montgomery. The play is still performed every year at the Charlottetown Festival, along with other Canadian musicals.

Stratford Festival

Canada's first professional theater began in a tent in 1953! Located in the town of Stratford, Ontario, this drama festival is now famous for its productions of plays written by William Shakespeare. The town itself is named after Shakespeare's birthplace in England. Today, the plays are performed in Stratford's three large theaters.

Shaw Festival

The Shaw Festival produces the plays of Irish **playwright** George Bernard Shaw and other works written during the period in which Shaw lived. These plays include musicals, mysteries, dramas, and comedies. The Shaw acting company performs in two theaters in the historic town of Niagara-on-the-Lake, Ontario.

(below) Live theater is thriving across Canada, from British Columbia to this production of Anne of Green Gables *in Charlottetown, Prince Edward Island.*

Cirque du Soleil

French Canadians express their cultural pride through a wide variety of arts. A good example of French Canada's culture is *Cirque du Soleil* or "Circus of the Sun." Based in Montréal, Québec, it is like no other circus in the world! *Cirque du Soleil* is a theater production and circus all in one. There are no animals in its acts; all the performers are human. Color, costumes, light, music, and drama are combined with traditional circus acts such as juggling, tightrope walking, and **trapeze**. This wonderful traveling show thrills and excites audiences throughout North America, Europe, and Japan.

(above) Every season a number of William Shakespeare's plays, such as the Merchant of Venice, *are showcased at the Stratford Festival.*

(right) The spectacular costumes and exciting acts of Cirque du Soleil *performers keep audiences on the edge of their seats.*

(above) Native Canadian playwright Tomson Highway.

(below) Mordecai Richler is one of Canada's most widely read authors.

Native Canadians were the first to tell stories and myths about Canada. For thousands of years, native children were educated by listening to stories told by their **elders**. Today, there are some well-known Native Canadian writers who are telling the ancient tales of their ancestors.

Native storytellers

One of Canada's favorite native authors is Tomson Highway. He was born in northern Manitoba on his father's **trapline**. Highway spoke only the Cree language until he was sent to a residential school at the age of six. Today, he still writes his plays and novels first in his native language, then translates them into English. *The Rez Sisters* and *Dry Lips Oughta Move to Kapuskasing* are two of Highway's most successful plays. His writings deal with the good and bad aspects of native communities.

Early writings

When European settlers came to Canada, they brought their own storytelling traditions. People entertained one another by telling stories and folktales. Some people wrote down their stories, and by doing so, contributed to Canadian recorded cultural history. Some of the earliest writing by European immigrants told of the harsh wilderness and difficulties of life in the rugged Canadian landscape. Susanna Moodie's book *Roughing it in the Bush* was published in the 1850s. It is a tale of life as a Canadian settler.

Canadian classics

There are many Canadian writers whose books are read by nearly every Canadian schoolchild. One such writer is Montréal-born novelist and journalist Mordecai Richler. His novels often reflect his own past growing up in Montreal. He is best known for his novel *The Apprenticeship of Duddy Kravitz*. He also wrote a popular children's book, *Jacob Two-Two Meets the Hooded Fang*.

Noted poets

Canada has produced a number of renowned poets. The famous war remembrance poem "In Flanders Fields" was written by a Canadian soldier named John McCrae during WW I. Leonard Cohen, a poet and musician, is another notable Canadian. His first book of poetry was published in 1956. Cohen later began writing music, and became a songwriter. He has also published several books.

A global perspective

Canada is a country of many immigrants, and Canadian literature often reflects the history and culture of other countries. Michael Ondaatje was born in Sri Lanka in 1943 and came to Canada in 1962. A poet and novelist, Ondaatje has won many awards for his writing. Some of his writings are about his own life, growing up in Sri Lanka and immigrating to Canada. He also writes about historical figures in his novels and poems. His book *The English Patient* was made into an Academy Award-winning movie in 1996.

(top) Canadian poet Leonard Cohen is also a songwriter and singer.

(below) Novelist Michael Ondaatje was born in Sri Lanka.

World renowned

Many Canadian writers are known around the world. Margaret Atwood is an author who has gained international attention. Her novel *The Handmaid's Tale*, was published in 25 countries. Many of her writings focus on women, social conditions, and Canadian identity. She has written numerous successful fiction books, as well as poetry, short stories, articles, and children's books. Atwood has won Canadian and international literary awards for her works.

(above) Internationally renown author Margaret Atwood.

For younger readers

Children's author Robert Munsch is famous worldwide for his hilarious books. *Stephanie's Ponytail*, *Paper Bag Princess*, and *Alligator Baby* are some of his books. Munsch first started telling stories while working with children at a daycare center. His stories were very popular, so he eventually wrote them down. Robert Munsch is now one of Canada's best-selling authors. His book *Love You Forever*, which is about the love between parents and children, has sold more than eighteen million copies!

Anne of Green Gables

Lucy Maude Montgomery was born in Prince Edward Island in 1874. She wrote the well-known "Anne of Green Gables" books, which follow the life of a spunky red-headed girl in Prince Edward Island. The stories of Anne Shirley have been so popular that they have been translated into 35 languages. Anne has been made into plays, films, stage musicals, and television series. Other series written by L. M. Montgomery are Rilla of Ingleside and Emily of New Moon. Montgomery's books appeal to people of all ages and cultures.

(above) Popular children's author Robert Munsch travels around North America telling stories.

(opposite page) Canada has two official languages, English and French. Many signs are written in both languages.

(below) This green-gabled house in Prince Edward Island was the basis of Lucy Maud Montgomery's "Anne" books.

The spoken word

Canada is officially a bilingual country. Bilingual means "two languages." Canada's two official languages are English and French. Almost 60 percent of Canadians speak English as their first language. About 23 percent speak French. There are almost 100 other languages spoken in Canada. Chinese, Italian, and German are the most commonly spoken languages, after English and French. There are also 53 native languages, including Cree, Inuktitut, Ojibwa, and Mi'kmaq.

Native words

Several words in the English language have come from native languages. **Igloo**, **parka**, canoe, and **muskeg** are all native words. Many place names in Canada are actually native names. The word "Canada" itself is thought to come from the **Iroquois** word "kanata," which means "village." Saskatchewan, Manitoba, Ontario, Québec, and Yukon are also derived from native words.

Canadian French

The French language was brought to Canada by fur-traders and settlers from France. Over time, the language has changed. The French spoken in Canada today is not exactly the same as the French spoken in France. French Canadians speak with a different accent than French people in France. Also, certain words have changed. For example, the word "car" is translated as *char* in Canada, but *auto* in France.

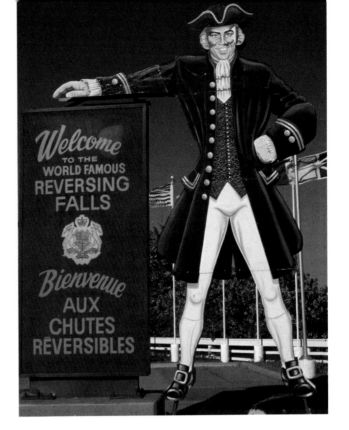

Zee or zed?

The English language was brought to North America by the British. In the United States, the language has changed into "American English." Canada, for the most part, continues to use "British English." One major difference between the two versions of English is the pronunciation of the letter "z." Americans say "zee," while Canadians say "zed." There are also differences in spelling. Words such as "color" and "honor" in the United States are spelled "colour" and "honour" in Canada. Words ending in "er" are often spelled with "re" instead. For example, "center" is spelled "centre."

English	French	Cree
Hello	Bonjour	ta'n(i)si
Goodbye	Au revoir	ki'htwa'm ka-wa'p(a)mit(i)n
How are you?	Comment ça va?	ta'n(i)si
I am fine	Ça va bien	m'on~(a) na'ntaw
Yes	Oui	e'he'
No	Non	mo'n~a
What is your name?	Comment t'appelles tu?	ta'n(i)si e's(i)n~ihka'soyan
Thank you	Merci	kinana'skomitin

Television and film

Most of the television and film that Canadians watch is produced by Americans. Even though these television shows and movies are American made, they are still "Canadian" in some ways. Many of the scenes are filmed in Canada's beautiful cities, mountains, and prairies!

Proudly Canadian

Canadian television networks realize the importance of showing programs that deal with national issues and provide Canadian role models. The government supports the music, filmmaking, and television programming produced by Canadians. These industries are growing quickly, and Canadian productions are winning international awards for their excellent quality.

The CBC

The Canadian Broadcasting Corporation (CBC) is an important part of Canadian culture. It is a government-owned network that provides radio and television broadcasting in both English and French. The CBC produces national news programs and **documentaries** as well as comedy and drama television programs reflecting Canadian issues.

The NFB

The National Film Board was formed in 1939. It produces documentaries, animated films, and dramatic films. These films are often shown at international film festivals and sometimes are more popular abroad than they are within Canada.

(above) A Canadian film crew gets ready to shoot their next scene. Canada's beautiful landscapes provide the setting for many modern-day movies, including Hollywood films!

Famous Canadians on screen

There has always been a steady stream of Canadian performers moving to the United States in order to further their careers. Mary Pickford was born in Toronto and started her career there at the age of five before moving to the United States. She acted in silent films in the early 1900s, and quickly became known as "America's sweetheart." Actor William Shatner, who stared as Captain Kirk in *Star Trek*, was also born in Canada. He started his career as a stage actor at the Stratford Festival in Ontario. He has continued to act in television and movies, becoming one of Canada's best known stars. Comedians Jim Carrey and Mike Myers are also Canadian. Today, some Canadian performers, such as actress Sarah Polley, choose to remain in Canada to help build Canada's performing arts industry.

Mainstream movies

Canada is sometimes called "Hollywood North" because many American film companies make movies there. The popular television show, *The X-files*, was filmed in Vancouver. Many American movies are also made in large urban centers such as Toronto and Montreal. Canadians also make feature films of their own. David Cronenberg is a well-known Canadian director whose films are known around the world. He makes his movies in Canada, often employing American stars as the actors. Atom Egoyan's artistic films are also popular internationally. His film *The Sweet Hereafter* won three prizes at the Cannes Film Festival in France.

(top) Mary Pickford, known as "America's sweetheart," was born in Canada.

(right) Famous comedian Jim Carrey is also a Canadian.

Canada is a nation of music lovers. Country, jazz, classical, and rock are among the musical choices of Canadians. The music of different cultures, such as Jamaican reggae, African-American rap, Celtic folk music, and French-Canadian songs, are also popular. Live music can be heard in crowded concert halls, stadiums, and night clubs across Canada.

Celtic music

Celtic music originates from the traditional music of Ireland, Scotland, and Wales. It was brought to Canada by immigrants from the United Kingdom. Many of the immigrants settled on Cape Breton Island, in the eastern province of Nova Scotia. Celtic music is still prominent in Cape Breton today, and can be heard on pipes, harps, fiddles, guitars, and pianos. Gatherings called ceilidhs (pronounced kay-leez) are parties where celtic bands play and people can sing along and dance.

French Canadian music

French Canadian folk music was influenced by many forms of music, such as celtic, blues, and jazz. Some folk songs have been passed down through generations. Songs are often about the social and political conditions of French Canadians. Piano, fiddle, accordion, organ, and sometimes guitar are the main instruments used to play French Canadian music. The reels and **jigs** are played in a fast tempo to encourage people to dance. The traditional folk music of Québec also influenced folk-rock artists of the 1970s, such as musician and poet Gilles Vigneault. He is one of Québec's best known *chansonniers*. His song *Mon Pays*, which means "my country" in French, is a favorite in the province.

The big names

Many Canadian musicians have gained international fame. French-Canadian singer Celine Dion has sold hundreds of millions of albums and performed all over the world. Well-known rock musician Neil Young grew up in Winnipeg, where he met fellow Canadian musicians Randy Bachman and Burton Cummings. Many of Neil Young's song lyrics describe his Canadian youth.

All that jazz

Canada's great jazz pianist, Oscar Peterson, has performed for audiences around the world. During his career, which spans more than 60 years, he has played with such great artists as Billie Holiday and Louis Armstrong. Peterson has received seven American Grammy Awards and numerous Canadian awards of recognition, including the **Order of Canada**. In 1997, he was awarded a Lifetime Achievement Award by the National Academy of Recording Arts.

Classical

Canada is proud of its classical musicians as well as its jazz and pop stars. Pianist Glen Gould was probably the most well known Canadian classical musician. His Goldberg Variations by Bach, recorded in 1955 and 1981, still stand as classics today. Canada has symphony orchestras in major cities from Nova Scotia to British Columbia. Ben Heppner, Richard Margison, and Michael Schade are Canada's three famous opera tenors.

Music festivals

Canadian music festivals are held throughout the country. These festivals are usually held outdoors in the summer and early fall. Some music festivals focus on one type of music, such as the Big Valley Jamboree in Camrose, Alberta, which is a country and western music festival. At this festival, not only do musicians showcase their talents, but log-pulling contests, rodeos, and craft vendors also keep visitors busy.

(opposite page, far left) An African-Canadian singer performs at the Montréal Jazz Festival.

(opposite page, left) French-Canadian Celine Dion is an internationally known musician.

(right) Summertime is the season for music festivals! Hillside festival in Guelph, Ontario, is one of the many Canadian music festivals that occur every year.

(above) Folk festivals were originally a chance for local musicians to show their talents to their communities.

Canadian art has its roots in the ancient traditional arts of the native peoples. The wonders of nature have inspired Native Canadian artists for generations. Native arts range from the tall totem poles of the west-coast Haida to the detailed masks of the Iroquois. The **Inuit** skill of carving figures from soapstone is thousands of years old. Native artists still use traditional methods to express themselves in powerful and lasting ways.

Kane and Krieghoff

Among Canada's early settlers were artists who sketched scenes of pioneer life. Paul Kane journeyed across Canada with the Hudson's Bay Company fur trading canoe fleet. Along the way, he painted pictures of native villages and herds of bison that wandered across the plains. Cornelius Krieghoff, a European painter who lived in Canada during the same period, recorded the life of the settlers living in Québec.

The Group of Seven

Canada's most famous art was created in the 1920s by the Group of Seven. This band of painters, which eventually included ten artists, portrayed the beauty of Canada's wilderness on canvas. These artists captured the spirit of every season in vivid colors and bold brush strokes. The Group of Seven artists were inspired by Tom Thomson, a gifted artist who painted the wonders of northern Ontario. Although Thomson died before the Group of Seven was formed, his paintings are similar in style and his name is always associated with the group.

William Kurelek

William Kurelek grew up on a farm in Alberta. As an adult, his paintings were influenced by his prairie roots, his Ukrainian upbringing, and his strong Christian faith. Kurelek created more than 1200 paintings of his childhood, which showed detailed scenes of everyday farm life.

Emily Carr

In the early twentieth century, Emily Carr recorded the vanishing native villages, houses, and totem poles of British Columbia through her art. She also painted forests, skies, and beaches in a strong, colorful style. Carr is still one of Canada's most revered artists.

Art today

Galleries showing the works of today's artists, sculptors, and photographers can be found in every city in Canada. The art can range from realistic paintings to modern abstract creations. Charles Pachter is a painter, printmaker, sculptor, and graphic artist who is known for his unique paintings of Canadian symbols such as moose, the flag, and mounties.

(above) Cornelius Krieghoff is known for his colorful, realistic paintings of French-Canadian settler life.

(opposite page) Traditional skills such as carving totem poles and soapstone figures are still practiced by many Native Canadians.

(above) This painting, called Sketch for the Jackpine, *was painted by Tom Thomson.*

Buildings and structures

While European and Asian buildings can be hundreds of years old, most Canadian buildings are much younger. Canada as a nation is less than two hundred years old, so even its oldest buildings are new by world standards. Over the past 50 years, thousands of new buildings have been erected across the country. Many of these structures are marvels of modern design and technology.

Canadian characteristics

Architecture often reflects a country's climate as well as the building materials that are available. In pioneer days, Canadian structures were built of wood, stone, and even **sod**. Today, bricks, concrete, and steel are used as building materials. Modern buildings are well **insulated** to keep Canadians warm during the cold winter season. Many buildings are also air conditioned so that residents will be more comfortable during the hot summers.

The buildings of Toronto

Toronto, Canada's largest city, contains some amazing buildings. The CN Tower is the world's tallest free-standing structure. Every year, thousands of people take the elevator ride to the top of the tower to enjoy the spectacular view of Toronto and Lake Ontario. The SkyDome is a modern, 31-story sports stadium with a **retractable** roof. Toronto City Hall consists of two curved buildings that stand out from the rectangular **skyscrapers** around them.

A shopper's dream

One of the biggest attractions in the city of Edmonton, Alberta, is the West Edmonton Mall. With over 800 stores, it is the world's largest shopping center. Adults and children can play in any of the mall's seven amusement parks, skate on the indoor ice rink, ride the fourteen-story-high roller coaster, or visit the sharks, dolphins, and other sea life at one of the aquariums.

Canadian Museum of Civilization

The Canadian Museum of Civilization in Hull, Québec, was designed by Native Canadian architect Douglas Cardinal. This museum is a large building with glass walls and huge copper domes. The museum contains various halls, presenting different parts of Canadian history. There is a Children's Museum, a Native Indian and Inuit Art Gallery, and a movie theater.

The National Gallery

The National Gallery of Canada in Ottawa is a blend of old and new architecture. It has an old-fashioned design, but is built with modern materials. Glass walls, flower-filled gardens, and lofty ceilings give visitors the feeling of being outdoors. The National Gallery contains one of the best collections of Canadian and European art in the country.

(above) The Canadian Museum of Civilization, located near the Ontario–Québec border, opened in 1989.

(opposite page) A spectacle of lights outlines Toronto's curved City Hall and the public skating rink in the foreground.

(below) The spectacular structure of the National Gallery is as much an example of art as the works displayed inside. Granite, wood, concrete, steel, and a lot of glass were combined to build this gallery.

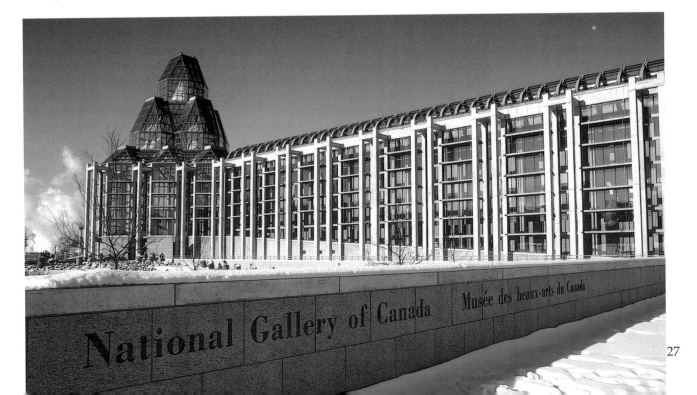

Clothing

There is no such thing as typical Canadian clothing because people in Canada wear a wide variety of styles. An Inuit in northern Canada might wear a parka and **mukluks**, while a businesswoman in Toronto might be dressed in a designer suit. A visitor to Canada could see several different styles of modern and traditional dress during a short walk down a Canadian city street. From miniskirts to sweatshirts to **saris**, nothing is unexpected.

Fashion

Fashion in Canada generally follows European and American trends. Clothing is often imported from the United States, Europe, and Asia. Although Canadian designers and clothing manufacturers face a competitive market, companies such as Roots and designers such as Alfred Sung have established worldwide success.

(right) Beadwork decorates native costmes.

(below) Canadian clothing styles are similar to European and American styles.

Native clothing

For some Native Canadians, wearing traditional clothing is a part of their daily life and culture. For others, traditional clothing is only worn for celebrations and ceremonies. Originally, native clothing was made of animal hides and fur. Garments were even sewn with thread made of animal **sinew**. Today, the Dene people of the Northwest Territories for example, still make moccasins and mittens of wolf fur and moosehide, and jackets of hareskin. The clothing is decorated with dyed porcupine quills and beads.

Mukluks and moccasins

Many native groups still make and wear moccasins and mukluks. Moccasins are like shoes, and mukluks are knee high, like boots. Both types of footwear are made from animal skins, and may have fur on the cuffs. They are lined with fur and often decorated with beads.

The practical parka

For the Inuit people, traditional clothing styles are an important part of life. Parkas are coats made of caribou or seal skin, and worn by the Inuit. The parkas are designed to provide insulation from wet and cold weather. Keeping warm and dry is important to the Inuit, who make their living hunting, trapping, and fishing in Canada's icy north. Originally, parkas for women had pouches for carrying babies. Parkas are often embroidered with beads.

A Canadian symbol

One classic piece of Canadian dress seen as a symbol of Canada is the uniform of the Royal Canadian Mounted Police (RCMP). The RCMP are also called the Mounties. The uniform is made up of a wide-brimmed hat, red tunic, and dark pants with a yellow stripe. Mounties from different cultural or religious backgrounds may slightly alter their uniforms. For example, Sikh Mounties are allowed to wear their **turbans** with the rest of the traditional Mountie uniform. The RCMP uniform dates back more than 100 years. Today, officers wear the scarlet tunic uniforms for ceremonial occasions only.

(above) Inuit wear clothing made of animal furs in order to survive in the cold climate of Arctic Canada.

(below) Two Royal Canadian Mounted Police officers in full uniform.

Myths and legends

Every country in the world has myths, **legends**, and stories that people read or tell one another. Myths are ancient tales that may use fictional characters and situations to teach truths about life. Myths and legends often teach values such as courage and honor, and explain the mysteries of nature. Here is an example of an Ojibwa native legend that has been passed on through many generations. It is a tale about the creation of North America.

How the world was made
Long ago the earth was covered by a great sea. It was home to swimming mammals, fish, birds, and reptiles. High above them in the heavens the Sky Woman lived all alone.

To make her happy, the Great Spirit sent a companion, but the companion left. Soon after, the Sky Woman gave birth to twins who were not at all alike. They fought and finally destroyed each other, and the Sky Woman was alone again. The Great Spirit then sent another companion and, as before, the companion left.

The water creatures felt sorry that the Sky Woman was lonely and wanted her to come down and join them. They persuaded a giant turtle to offer his back as a resting place. The Sky Woman accepted the offer. Once settled, she asked the animals to dive down into the water and bring up some dirt from the bottom of the ocean.

The animals wanted to please the Sky Woman. The beaver was the first to dive deep into the sea. Soon he surfaced, out of breath but with no soil. The otter and **marten** each took a turn but returned to the surface empty-handed. Finally, the **muskrat** volunteered. The other creatures laughed at him. They doubted that this animal was any match for the task, but the little muskrat wanted to try. Down, down he went. He did not surface for a long time. The others became very worried. Just when they had given up hope for return of their friend, the muskrat floated to the surface, close to death. Clutched in his tiny paws was a small bit of soil.

The Sky Woman painted the turtle's back with this soil. She breathed upon the soil, and it began to grow until it became a huge island. The Ojibwa people call this land "The Island of the Great Turtle." Other people call it North America.

Glossary

ancestor A person from whom one is descended

architecture The science, art, or profession of designing, planning, and constructing buildings

Arctic The region surrounding the North Pole

band A native group that manages its own affairs

Buddhism A religion founded by Buddha, an ancient religious leader from India

chansonniers A French-Canadian term meaning singer

Christianity A religion based on the teachings of Jesus Christ, whom Christians believe is the son of God

cultural mosaic A term used to describe Canada as a country made up of people who come from different cultural backgrounds

denomination A religious group that is a branch or form of a larger religious group

documentary A program or film that presents the facts of a particular subject

elder A senior member of a Native group

grant A sum of money given by the Canadian government

heritage The customs, achievements, and history passed on from earlier generations

Hinduism An ancient East Indian religion based on holy books called the *Vedas*

igloo A dwelling used by natives in the north that is made from snow and ice

immigrant A person who settles in a new country

insulate To keep warm

Inuit Native people who live in Canada's Arctic

Iroquois A group of Native nations in southeastern Ontario and southern Québec

Islam A religion founded by the prophet Muhammad. Followers of Islam are called Muslims

jig A fast, lively dance

legend A story passed down through the years

marten A small weasel-like animal

mukluk A high boot with thick soles

multiculturalism The policy of accepting many cultures within one country

muskeg A swamp covered with moss

muskrat A large swimming rodent

Order of Canada The highest Canadian award given for special achievements

parka A long, warm coat

playwright A person who writes plays

reservation An area of land put aside by the government for native use

retractable Describing something that opens and closes

sari A dress-like garment worn by East Indian women

shaman A native healer and spiritual leader

Sikhism An East Indian religion based on the teachings of a man named Guru Nanak

sinew The tissue that connects muscles and bones

skyscraper A very tall building

sod A strip of grass and soil

traditions Long-held customs or beliefs

trapeze A short, swinging horizontal bar suspended from two ropes

trapline The area where animal traps are set up

turban A length of cloth wrapped around the head that symbolizes devotion to a Sikh religion

Index

Anne of Green Gables 14, 18
architecture 4, 26–27
art 4, 5, 24–25, 27
artists 24–25
Atwood, Margaret 17
authors 16, 17, 18
ballet 13
Canadian Broadcasting Corporation (CBC) 20
Canadian Museum of Civilization 27
caribana 10, 11
Carr, Emily 25
Carrey, Jim 21
Charlottetown Festival 14
Cirque du Soleil 15
clothing 4, 7, 28
CN Tower 26
Cohen, Leonard 17

Cree language 19
Cronenberg, David 21
dance 4, 12–15, 22
Dion, Celine 22
Egoyan, Atom 21
festivals 4, 8–11, 12, 14, 15, 20, 21, 23
film 18, 20–21
French Canadians 8, 15, 19, 22
Group of Seven 24
Highway, Tomson 16
holidays 8–11
Inuit 24, 27, 28, 29
Kane, Paul 24
Krieghoff, Cornelius 24, 25
Kurelek, William 24
language 4, 19
legends 30–31
literature 4, 5, 16–19

Montgomery, Lucy Maud 14, 18
Montréal 7, 10, 13, 15, 16, 23
Moodie, Susanna 16
movies *see* film
multiculturalism 5
Munsch, Robert 18
music 4, 5, 9, 10, 12, 13, 15, 17, 20, 22–23
musicals 13, 14, 18
Myers, Mike 21
myths *see* legends
National Ballet of Canada 13
National Film Board (NFB) 20
National Gallery of Canada 27
native peoples 4, 6, 12, 16, 19, 24, 25, 27, 29, 30
Ondaatje, Michael 17
Ottawa 13, 17, 27

Pachter, Charles 25
Peterson, Oscar 22
Pickford, Mary 21
religion 4, 6–7
Richler, Mordecai 16
Royal Canadian Mounted Police (RCMP) 29
Shatner, William 21
Shaw Festival 14
SkyDome 26
Stratford Festival 14, 15
television 5, 18, 20–21
theater 4, 5, 12–15
Thomson, Tom 24, 25
Toronto 7, 10, 13, 26, 27, 28
Vancouver 13
Vigneault, Gilles 22
West Edmonton Mall 27
Young, Neil 22

1 2 3 4 5 6 7 8 9 0 Printed in the USA 0 9 8 7 6 5 4 3 2 1